London

To Noel and Lynne,
thank you for being my first home
in London and giving me the best start
to my first London adventure.

London

THROUGH A FASHION EYE

Megan Hess

Hardie Grant

BOOKS

Contents

Introduction

There's a particular style of wit and charm that is characteristic to London's streets. The fashion here has such a distinct aesthetic that you just don't find anywhere else – a mixture of their aristocratic heritage with the slightly gritty modern punk look that only the British really pull off. It's a wonderful place to travel if you love fashion.

London is where I first began illustrating fashion, so I will always credit this city as being a place that sparked my creative journey. It's where I first realised that anything in an artistic field was possible.

When I first moved to London in my twenties, I found a job in a little retail boutique and quickly fell in love with the city. I was on a tight budget, but there was still so much to see and do. I would spend my lunchbreaks wandering in front of incredible architecture and famous paintings in the free galleries, feeding my creative soul, or gazing in the windows of shops such as Burberry. I didn't buy a *thing*, but I still adored soaking up all the fashion scene had to offer.

Starting work in creative agencies, I learned a huge amount about the London fashion industry. I remember being taken to visit Savile Row, which felt like stepping into a magical world of heritage tailoring – with all that walnut wood, giant bookshelves, leather couches and exquisite craftsmanship. Later, I worked on art direction for Liberty department store, I was involved in all kinds of wild creative projects – like photoshoots with models on elephants!

Ever since then, I've always loved going back to London. I've been able to experience the city in a particularly fabulous way, being invited to sketch private showings at Dior Couture London or being artist-in-residence for the incredible Lanesborough Hotel. I can eat and stay at places I never could when I first moved there, but what I love about London remains the same: that uniquely British aesthetic and craftsmanship.

In this book, I've gathered together my favourite spots for fashion-loving travellers in London. I hope it helps you to fall in love with this city too.

My favourite things ...

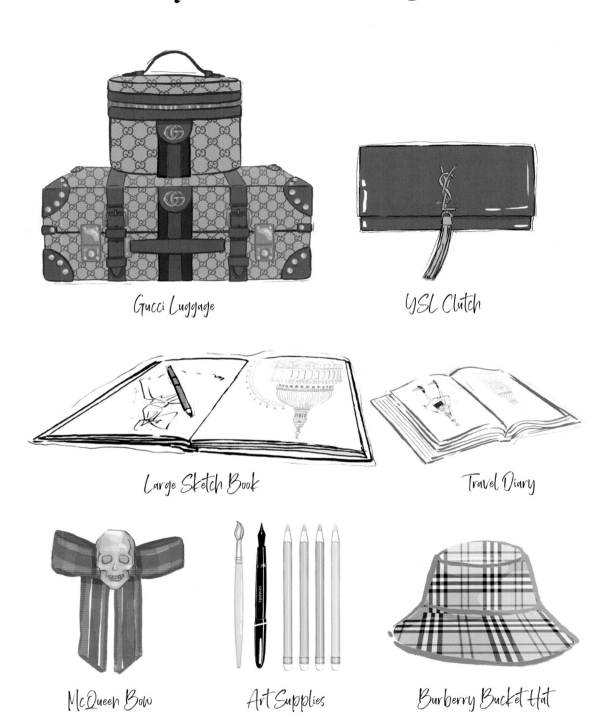

Gucci Luggage

YSL Clutch

Large Sketch Book

Travel Diary

McQueen Bow

Art Supplies

Burberry Bucket Hat

... to pack for London

Party Shoes

Valentino Rockstuds

Daywear Dress

Favourite Fragrance

Lipstick

Umbrella

Statement Earrings

Gucci Diana Bag

My favourite ensembles ...

Visiting
the Galleries

Shopping on
New Bond Street

An Engagement
at the Palace

... for London occasions

Exploring
Mayfair

Dinner &
Cocktails

A Night at
the Royal Opera

1

Do/
Play

National Gallery

TRAFALGAR SQUARE,
WESTMINSTER

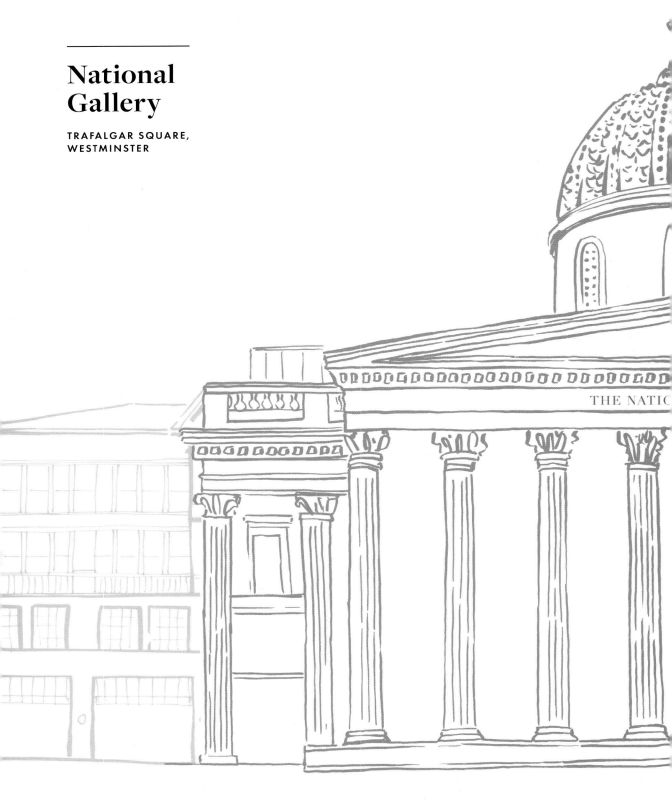

THE NATIO

Before I step through the main entrance of London's National Gallery, I like to look up at the towering, pillared portico entrance and appreciate the grandeur of the architecture. Once inside, visitors can see original artworks by greats like van Gogh, Turner, Monet and Da Vinci – the National Gallery has a vast collection of paintings dating back to the thirteenth century, organised chronologically through the various art movements. Entry to the main galleries is free, but don't forget to check if you're interested in booking into their special exhibitions, events and creative sessions. There's always something different happening here.

Fashion and Textile Museum

83 BERMONDSEY STREET, SOUTHWARK

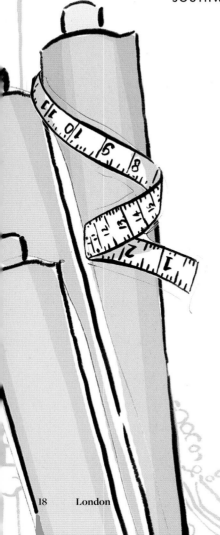

A small but beautifully crafted museum exploring the past, present and future of textiles, founded by fashion legend Dame Zandra Rhodes. The bright orange exterior gives way to a series of spaces with a rotating program of exhibitions that deep-dive into particular elements of fashion design, industry and craftsmanship, such as 'The Boutique in 1960s Counterculture' or '150 Years of the Royal School of Needlework'. Their permanent collection is accessible to researchers by arrangement, and they also offer a range of workshops and talks, so a visit here can be an immersive fashion learning experience.

Fashion
and Textile
Museum

Victoria and Albert Museum

CROMWELL ROAD, SOUTH KENSINGTON

The concept for the Victoria and Albert Museum grew out of the Great Exhibition in 1851, when the Crystal Palace in Hyde Park hosted global exhibitions by the world's designers. Prince Albert imagined a permanent public design museum. The current V&A building was completed in 1857, and is a fashion and design history mecca. From the arched main entrance and domed marble foyer, the museum splits into seven miles of themed galleries, so it's worth planning your visit! The V&A holds the most comprehensive collection of dresses in the world, and their footwear collection is a journey through history, from Egyptian shoes originating from 1550 BC to beaded Dolce & Gabbana boots. Similarly, their jewellery collection tells the story of how people have decorated themselves for thousands of years. The Victoria and Albert is also responsible for their fascinating and free 'Fashion in Motion' series, putting historic fashion on the catwalk.

National Portrait Gallery

ST MARTIN'S PLACE, WESTMINSTER

Among the National Portrait Gallery's more than 220,000 works are portraits of fashion greats such as Jimmy Choo, Jean Paul Gaultier, Laura Ashley, Vivienne Westwood and Manolo Blahnik. The gallery also holds no less than fifty-three portraits of one of my style idols, Audrey Hepburn. Even when the subjects aren't famous for fashion, the subject's fashion choices can say a lot about them and their historical era. Entry is free, so when I first moved to London I would visit here on my lunchbreaks, finding inspiration in both the beautiful artworks and the remarkable people they celebrate.

Tate Modern

BANKSIDE,
SOUTHWARK

The Tate Modern, on the banks of the River Thames, is in a huge nineteenth-century brick building that used to be the Bankside Power Station. The designer of the original building was architect Sir Giles Gilbert Scott, who also designed the classic British red telephone box we all know and love. Inside, this towering, cavernous space houses the United Kingdom's national collection of modern and contemporary art, including works by artists such as Picasso, Dalí and Warhol. With its immense free installations and immersive contemporary works, it's no surprise that this is one of London's most popular museums. The viewing platform on the tenth floor is also worth a peek, with stunning views of the city skyline.

London
Library

14 ST JAMES'S SQUARE,
ST JAMES'S

THE
LONDON
LIBRARY

COUTURE

CHANEL

FASHION

Dior

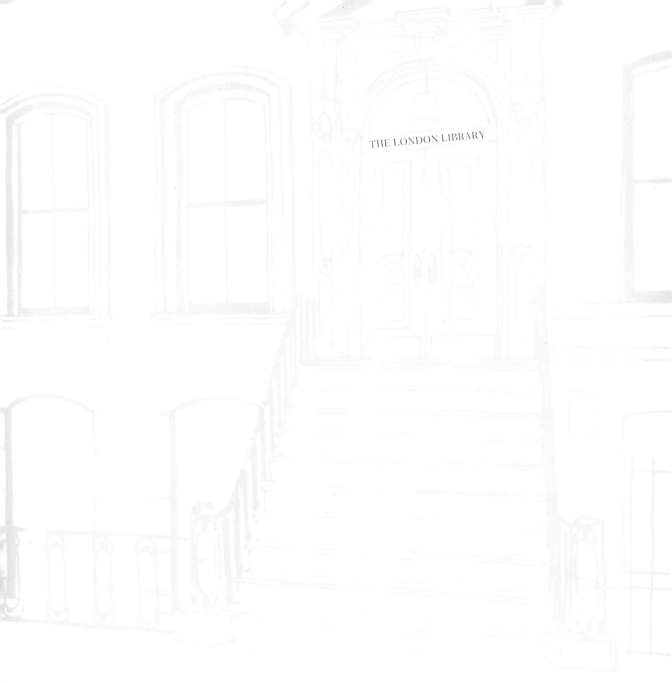

THE LONDON LIBRARY

There's something so romantic about labyrinths of old wooden bookcases, with little ladders leading up to the top shelves. The London Library was founded in 1841, when there were no other lending libraries in London, and has become a special place for writers and creators through history, such as Virginia Woolf and Agatha Christie. In 2022, Helena Bonham Carter became president, and I imagine her eccentric vintage style fits perfectly among the stacks of gold-inlayed, leatherbound books, some of which still have shrapnel damage from bombings during World War II. London Library has a private membership system, so you need to email them a few days early to request a ticket, which may take seventy-two hours to process, but it's worth it to marvel at more than a million books across seventeen miles (approximately 27 kilometres) of shelves!

Hyde Park

WESTMINSTER

One of the wonderful things about Central London is its huge public green spaces. Hyde Park is the largest of the Royal Parks in Central London and has something to discover around every corner, with columned archways, intricate memorials, and the expansive Serpentine Lake. I love any opportunity to sketch flowers, and the Hyde Park Rose Garden is perfect for this, as it bursts with blooms, especially in early summer. Ride a bike along Hyde Park's tree-lined pathways and bring a picnic to enjoy in the sunshine (if you're lucky)! Or visit in winter for the Hyde Park Winter Wonderland, which lights up the long nights with fairground rides, ice skating and Christmas cheer.

Walk along the Thames

A wander along the famous river at the heart of London is an opportunity to spot many of the city's distinctive sights. I like to start at the Westminster Bridge, on the aptly named Queen's Walk promenade, looking across the Thames at the Houses of Parliament with Big Ben at one end. The lacy gothic details of this Great Clock are a pleasure to sketch, and it's especially pretty lit up at night. Heading east along the river, the path goes directly beneath

the London Eye. If you decide to brave the queues and ascend into the sky, the observation pods will give you 360-degree views to spot many of London's landmarks, like Buckingham Palace, Westminster Abbey and the Tower of London. Follow the river from here for another hour or so to reach the beautiful Tower Bridge, passing the Tate Modern and Borough Markets along the way.

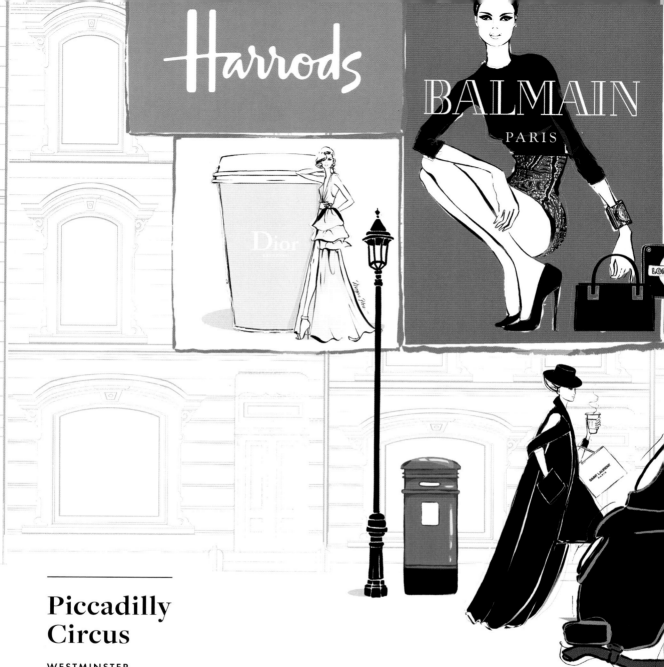

Piccadilly Circus

WESTMINSTER

Piccadilly Circus is one of the busiest road junctions in London, connecting Regent Street, Shaftesbury Avenue, Coventry Street, Glasshouse Street and Haymarket, with, of course, Piccadilly's own underground tube station. They say the name 'Piccadilly' comes from a local seventeenth-century tailor who made frilled collars called piccadills. This is the spot where theatre, shopping, restaurants and sightseeing collide, full of tourists during the day, and crowded with partygoers well into the night. Piccadilly Circus is famously lit up with huge neon billboards, a bit like New York's Times Square, and people often meet at the steps under the statue of Eros, to appreciate the lights before heading off to explore the nearby shopping and entertainment hotspots.

Covent
Garden
Piazza

**CRANBOURN STREET,
COVENT GARDEN**

Covent Garden Piazza was once a huge and bustling fruit and flower market. It's famously where we first meet Audrey Hepburn's Eliza in the movie *My Fair Lady*, selling bunches of violets on the street and singing 'Wouldn't it be loverly'. Now it is the perfect spot to wander through quaint arcades, discovering beautiful boutiques (Dior Beauty and Chanel both have little boutiques there), galleries, cafes and restaurants, or appreciating the architecture of the surrounding St Paul's Church, Royal Opera House and Theatre Royal. Outside the theatres, wild and vibrant street performers regularly turn the piazza into a stage.

BUCK

Buckingham Palace

....

**ENTER THROUGH THE ROYAL MEWS
BUCKINGHAM PALACE ROAD,
WESTMINSTER**

What could be more 'London' than a visit to Buckingham Palace? The state rooms are full of sumptuous detail: gilded furniture and thick red carpets, with priceless artwork on the walls and royal tiaras on display. I love the White Drawing Room, with its gold-and-white ceiling and secret doorway to the Royal Closet, and the pretty Music Room, which has blue columns and a domed ceiling. Because this is a working palace, tour tickets are only available at particular times of year and there's no guarantee you'll get to see all nineteen state rooms, as some might be in use when you visit. But on the plus side, you never know if there might be a princess in the next room!

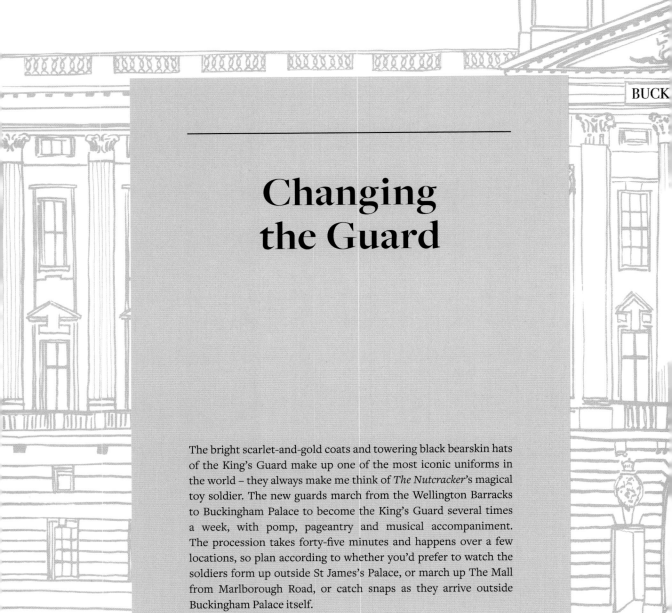

BUCK

Changing
the Guard

The bright scarlet-and-gold coats and towering black bearskin hats of the King's Guard make up one of the most iconic uniforms in the world – they always make me think of *The Nutcracker*'s magical toy soldier. The new guards march from the Wellington Barracks to Buckingham Palace to become the King's Guard several times a week, with pomp, pageantry and musical accompaniment. The procession takes forty-five minutes and happens over a few locations, so plan according to whether you'd prefer to watch the soldiers form up outside St James's Palace, or march up The Mall from Marlborough Road, or catch snaps as they arrive outside Buckingham Palace itself.

ALACE

Royal Opera House

**BOW STREET,
COVENT GARDEN**

The Royal Opera House is in London's West End, also affectionately known as 'Theatreland'. The Opera House itself is beautiful from both inside and out, with its huge glazed façade and cavernous balconied interior featuring sumptuous red velvet and gold trimmings. It's the home of both The Royal Ballet and The Royal Opera, and is perfect for a night enjoying one of their classic or contemporary performances, marvelling over the skilled artists as well as costumes full of rigorously designed theatrical detail. The Royal Opera House has several bars and restaurants and also offers various backstage tours and experiences. While you're here, check out what's playing at the other West End theatres or take a backstage tour of the National Theatre, where you can get inspired by the design of stage sets, props and costumes.

Shakespeare's Globe

21 NEW GLOBE WALK, BANKSIDE, SOUTHWARK

The original Globe theatre was built in 1599 by the Lord Chamberlain's Men, the theatre company that included a certain playwright by the name of William Shakespeare. It was destroyed twice, but was reconstructed in the 1990s as close as possible to the original design. With its hand-cut English oak, whitewashed lime plaster walls and thatched roof, this open-air theatre is like stepping back in history. Shakespeare's classics like *Hamlet*, *Macbeth* and *The Tempest* were all first performed at the Globe. The theatre now runs a program of Shakespeare, renaissance and contemporary shows, all with incredible costume designs of course. Audiences sit in balconied wooden galleries all around the outdoor stage, and the show must go on, even if it's snowing, so plan your own outfit accordingly!

London
Fashion Week

Alongside Paris, New York and Milan, London is one of the 'big four' fashion weeks. It has traditionally been held at Somerset House, on the Strand overlooking the Thames, with various shows in different locations across London. While this is

an invite-only industry event, it's followed by the London Fashion Week Festival, featuring ticketed catwalk shows by top designers, talks by industry experts and the opportunity to shop some of the designer collections at exclusive prices. Even if you aren't attending any of the shows, London is abuzz during fashion week, and bars and hotels around the venues are full of models, designers and buyers. I love finding a corner where I can sip a coffee or a cocktail and watch the fashion world go by.

CHELSEA

Chelsea Flower Show

ENTER VIA LONDON GATE,
ROYAL HOSPITAL ROAD,
CHELSEA

Each May, designer gardens take over the grounds of the Royal Hospital in Chelsea for this astonishing floral extravaganza, put on by the Royal Horticultural Society. Take time to appreciate the creativity on show, the fresh flowery scents, and of course the sheer beauty of the blooms. It's a prestigious event, with fashion A-listers and other celebrities making appearances, even royals – Queen Elizabeth II attended around fifty times during her long reign. If you can't obtain tickets, it's still worth wandering around nearby Chelsea and Belgravia, where shopfronts and restaurants join the celebrations with glorious floral displays.

The Lanesborough Spa

2 LANESBOROUGH PLACE, KNIGHTSBRIDGE

The Lanesborough Club & Spa has been called London's best hotel spa, and I don't disagree. This decadent sanctuary of deep relaxation features a stunning Grecian-style pool, a dramatic black-tiled dry sauna and steam room, and its own restaurant. Fitted out in marble, silk wallpaper, leather upholstery and peacock-blue satin, it's a treat for the eye, while you care for your body with a variety of indulgent treatments.

Annabel's

46 BERKELEY SQUARE,
MAYFAIR

The interior design of this exclusive private club is incredible. Entering each room is like crossing into a different fantasy universe, each with its own distinct feeling of intimate glamour. The ladies' bathrooms might actually be my favourite room – a lavish fairyland of pink marble, mother-of-pearl and florals. If you aren't planning to become a member, you can still walk past the building in Mayfair and be inspired by their stunning and ever-changing façade. The whole building regularly transforms – from a gingerbread house, to a Halloween arachnophobe's nightmare, to a glittering carousel – in an abundant display of creativity.

GALLERY

LONDON BRIDGE

Gallery hopping

As well as the major art institutions, London is full of smaller galleries, where emerging contemporary artists show their latest works. I love spending a day wandering from gallery to gallery, looking at emerging trends and discovering new and exciting aesthetics. London's West End, especially Covent Garden, is wonderful for galleries such as Clarendon Fine Art and Castle Fine Art and is also packed with fantastic pubs and restaurants to explore along the way. Portobello Road and surrounding Notting Hill are also home to Maddox Gallery and Select Gallery and many more. London's vibrant art scene offers something for everyone, and I always leave feeling inspired by the talent bubbling here – and perhaps with a special piece for my own home or studio.

2

Shop

Jo Malone London

101 REGENT STREET, SOHO

From making perfume with flowers in her kitchen as a little girl, Jo Malone went on to establish her eponymous brand, renowned for its opulent fragrances, candles, and bath products. With scents inspired by her own memories, Jo Malone's fragrances evoke a rich feeling of nature's beauty.

Now under the ownership of Estée Lauder, the brand has flourished, with numerous outlets in London, including their global flagship store on Regent Street, and a gorgeous boutique in Covent Garden. Their gift-wrapping service is perfection, and you may choose to schedule an appointment to have your perfume or bath oil bottles personally engraved.

JO MALONE
LONDON

Stephen Jones Millinery

36 GREAT QUEEN STREET, COVENT GARDEN

In the early 80s Stephen Jones was one of the Blitz Kids, regulars at the legendary Blitz nightclub, which launched the New Romantic movement. The club was a hub for creative experimentation by local arts students like Jones and was famous for its androgynous glamour and strict dress code. Boy George worked at the Blitz's cloakroom and was an early supporter of Jones. Jones established a millinery salon in Covent Garden and went on to make hats for Princess Diana and collaborate with luminaries Vivienne Westwood and Jean Paul Gaultier. His exceptional talent led to an OBE (Order of the British Empire) for services to fashion and his appointment as the first artistic director of hats at Christian Dior. A visit to his boutique in Covent Garden – a treasure trove of contemporary design history – is an absolute joy.

Harrods

87–135 BROMPTON ROAD,
KNIGHTSBRIDGE

No visit to London is complete without stopping at Harrods. This legendary department store is world-renowned for its high-end fashion offerings, and hosts an impressive selection of designer labels such as Burberry, Chanel, Gucci and its own Harrods fashion line. Harrods also has incredible food halls, where you might create your own bespoke tea blend or listen for

the bell that rings whenever fresh bread comes out of the ovens. Don't forget to check out the Harrods pop-up fashion cafes, which have included Prada, Dior and Jimmy Choo cafes in the past. The store's window displays are always spectacular and the interiors are similarly gorgeous, especially their famous Egyptian Escalator.

Selfridges

400 OXFORD STREET, MARYLEBONE

Selfridges on Oxford Street is the second-largest department store in the UK after Harrods. The store opened in 1909, and founder Harry Gordon Selfridge is known for transforming the shopping experience into a pleasurable activity. He focussed on making his store a comfortable public space, where women felt safe and shopping was convenient, with merchandise displayed so it was easy to examine. These retail techniques, revolutionary at the time, have become standards we now expect on our shopping expeditions. Selfridges offer an enormous range of brands, including one of my favourite London-based designers, Mary Katrantzou, 'the queen of print', whose creations have been worn by fashion leaders like Michelle Obama, Lupita Nyong'o and Cate Blanchett.

Oscar Wilde once said, 'Liberty is the chosen resort of the artistic shopper', and who are we to argue? The vast mock-Tudor building, with its charming crisscross of dark timber beams against white plaster and windowpanes, feels very English, and well deserves its heritage listing. Visiting Liberty always reminds me of my early days working there as an Art Director, which were so full of learning and inspiration for me. Liberty has a dedicated in-house studio and is known for its hand-painted fabrics and bold floral prints. It has a history of collaborative projects, from textile legends like William Morris to fashion royalty like Yves Saint Laurent, and is also known for championing young designers at the start of their careers.

Harvey Nichols

109–125 KNIGHTSBRIDGE,
KNIGHTSBRIDGE

Since it opened 1831, Harvey Nichols department store has gained a reputation for its curated collections of prestigious brands. Their grand red-and-cream brick corner building houses several storeys of women's, men's and children's fashion, beauty products, fine wine and luxury goods. Princess Diana used to be a regular client here, with a special place she liked to reserve at the back of the restaurant.

HARVEY NICHOLS

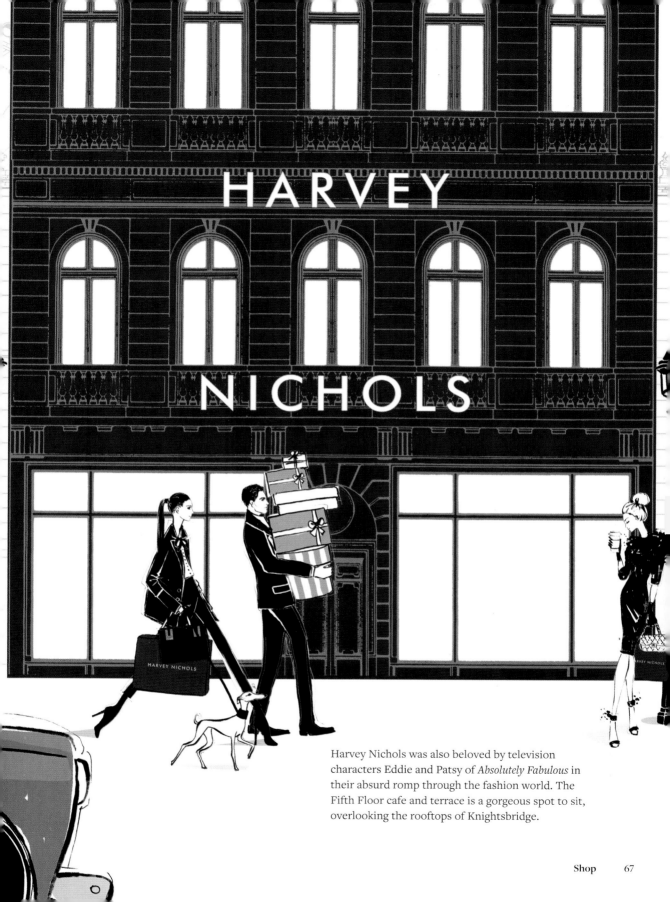

Harvey Nichols was also beloved by television characters Eddie and Patsy of *Absolutely Fabulous* in their absurd romp through the fashion world. The Fifth Floor cafe and terrace is a gorgeous spot to sit, overlooking the rooftops of Knightsbridge.

Fortnum
& Mason

181 PICCADILLY,
ST JAMES'S

William Fortnum was a footman in Queen Anne's household and Hugh Mason was his landlord, and the grocery store the two opened together soon became well known for supplying high-quality food. Since then, Fortnum & Mason has developed into an elegant department store, but where it really shines is still its provisions, from specialty biscuits to luxury hampers.

Wander past the stunning window displays and up the gilded curve of their grand spiral stairs, and stock up with chocolates and nibbles for a Hyde Park picnic or to pack in your suitcase. Fortnum & Mason is also one of London's famous destinations for afternoon tea, and their Diamond Jubilee Tea Salon on the fourth floor was opened by Queen Elizabeth II.

Hatchards

187 PICCADILLY,
ST JAMES'S

Hatchards was founded in 1797, making it the oldest bookshop in the UK.
It has been at the same prestigious location on Piccadilly, next to Fortnum
& Mason and across the road from the Royal Academy of Arts, since 1801.
One of the first ever customers on the Hatchards register was Queen
Charlotte, the wife of King George III, and the store still holds no less than
three Royal Warrants, meaning this is the official supplier of books to the
royal household. Hatchards is also known for being Oscar Wilde's favourite
bookshop and today the ground floor main table, where he used to sign his
books, is known as Oscar's table. I love browsing the towering oak shelves
and mahogany table displays, looking for my next holiday read. Hatchards
also has a store at St Pancras Station, just in case you're looking for
something fresh to read on a train trip under the channel to Europe.

Browns

**39 BROOK STREET,
MAYFAIR**

Founded by Joan Burstein (affectionately known to the fashion industry as Mrs B) and her husband Sidney, luxury boutique Browns is renowned for launching the careers of amazing designers like Alexander McQueen and Hussein Chalayan. They have also introduced a multitude of international designers to London, including Missoni, Ralph Lauren, Donna Karan and Alaïa. In 2021 they moved their flagship to a stunning building on Brook Street, Mayfair. The interior design contrasts heritage features like Flemish paintings with sleek modern steel fixtures to create a seamlessly contemporary ambiance. Browns is now owned by Farfetch, who have added a restaurant, wellness parlour and augmented reality elements to this remarkable shopping experience.

Matchesfashion

**5 CARLOS PLACE,
MAYFAIR**

Matchesfashion delivers a boutique shopping experience. The store – a converted five-storey Mayfair townhouse – feels both splendid and lived-in, designed to evoke the home of a luxurious, well-travelled couple. There are two floors of private shopping suites and racks featuring established and innovative designers, from Prada and Gucci to Halpern and Wales Bonner. They also offer another standout local label, Susie Cave's Vampire's Wife, which epitomises a certain dark, romantic British style and was famously worn by Kate Middleton for her first official joint portrait with her husband.

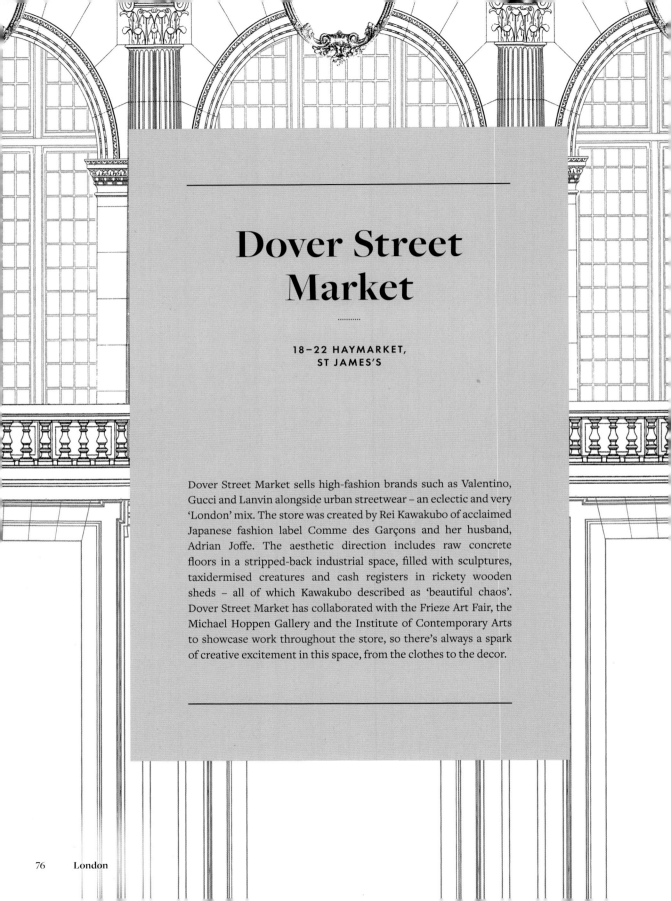

Dover Street Market

··········

**18–22 HAYMARKET,
ST JAMES'S**

Dover Street Market sells high-fashion brands such as Valentino, Gucci and Lanvin alongside urban streetwear – an eclectic and very 'London' mix. The store was created by Rei Kawakubo of acclaimed Japanese fashion label Comme des Garçons and her husband, Adrian Joffe. The aesthetic direction includes raw concrete floors in a stripped-back industrial space, filled with sculptures, taxidermised creatures and cash registers in rickety wooden sheds – all of which Kawakubo described as 'beautiful chaos'. Dover Street Market has collaborated with the Frieze Art Fair, the Michael Hoppen Gallery and the Institute of Contemporary Arts to showcase work throughout the store, so there's always a spark of creative excitement in this space, from the clothes to the decor.

Burberry

121 REGENT STREET,
MAYFAIR

I remember being a young woman exploring London for the first time and standing in front of the Burberry windows, just soaking in their style. This classic British brand was founded back in 1856 and has a strong heritage as makers of high-quality outerwear – such high quality, in fact, that they outfitted early expeditions to the South Pole and Antarctica. Burberry are known for their trench coats, cashmere scarves and of course the signature Burberry check. Their Regent Street store offers monogramming and in-store tailoring.

Vivienne Westwood

44 CONDUIT STREET, MAYFAIR

Queen of fantastical couture Vivienne Westwood has a history of punk and a flair for the outlandish. She entered the fashion world by opening her shop Let it Rock with Sex Pistols manager Malcolm McLaren on King's Road in London in the 1970s. Her zips, safety pins, leather and ripped t-shirts defined the radical subculture at that time and eventually made their way into mainstream fashion. Westwood is known for the MacAndreas tartan she designed and named in honour of her husband, and her distinctly British designs have been worn by everyone from Helena Bonham Carter to Kate Middleton to Sarah Jessica Parker (Carrie Bradshaw's billowing corseted wedding dress was classic Westwood). Her 44 Conduit Street flagship store houses the main Gold Label line, the more casual Anglomania and a range of accessories, while Vivienne Westwood Man is across the road at number 18.

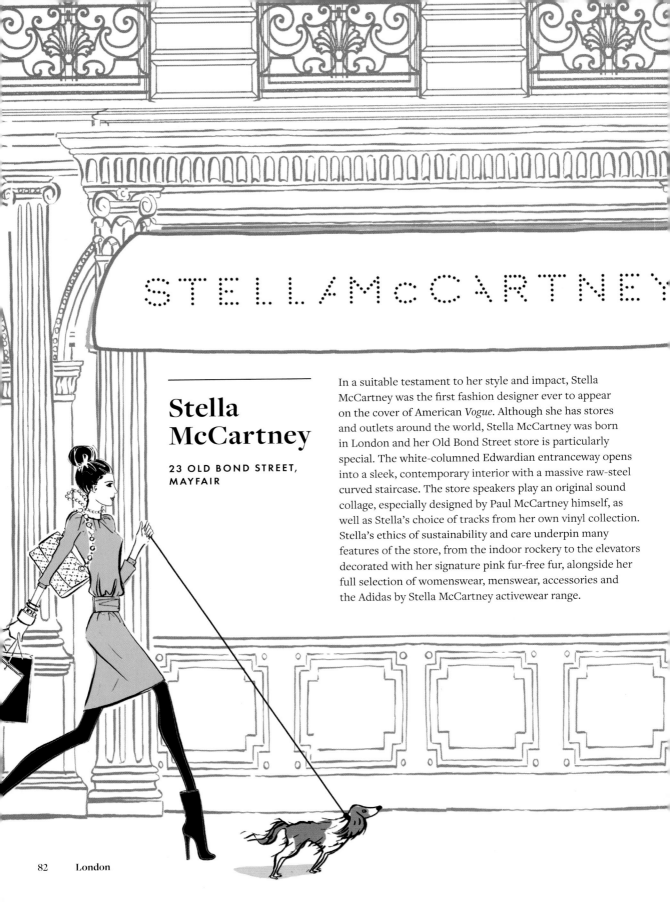

STELLA McCARTNEY

Stella McCartney

23 OLD BOND STREET, MAYFAIR

In a suitable testament to her style and impact, Stella McCartney was the first fashion designer ever to appear on the cover of American *Vogue*. Although she has stores and outlets around the world, Stella McCartney was born in London and her Old Bond Street store is particularly special. The white-columned Edwardian entranceway opens into a sleek, contemporary interior with a massive raw-steel curved staircase. The store speakers play an original sound collage, especially designed by Paul McCartney himself, as well as Stella's choice of tracks from her own vinyl collection. Stella's ethics of sustainability and care underpin many features of the store, from the indoor rockery to the elevators decorated with her signature pink fur-free fur, alongside her full selection of womenswear, menswear, accessories and the Adidas by Stella McCartney activewear range.

ALEXANDER McQUEEN

Alexander McQueen

27 OLD BOND STREET, MAYFAIR

Alexander McQueen is remembered as a visionary of fashion. His controversial designs and provocative fashion shows referenced the destructive forces of both nature and humanity. His dramatic work mixes Victorian, Gothic and Celtic with elements of leather, lace and the tartan that references his Scots heritage. When he passed away in 2010, his long-time assistant, Sarah Burton, was made creative director of the brand. A year later, Kate Middleton wore a Sarah Burton dress for her wedding in a tribute to British design. The Alexander McQueen flagship store in Old Bond Street has an archive and experiential space on the top floor, dedicated to the label's work in process, stories, team and materials, with a program of talks and exhibitions. It's wonderful to be immersed in the making of fashion history.

Erdem

**70 SOUTH
AUDLEY STREET,
MAYFAIR**

British designer Erdem Moralıoğlu creates feminine pieces characterised by elegant silhouettes, flowing silk and floral prints. His first ever collection was snapped up by Harrods, and the likes of Anna Wintour, Nicole Kidman and the Duchess of Cambridge have all worn and endorsed his work. He has even designed for The Royal Ballet, and his recent collaboration with de Gournay wallpapers is floral romantic perfection. His first store in Mayfair is designed to feel as though it were inhabited by Erdem's muse, 'a woman who is both unafraid of the world and one with it', and features beautiful powder-blue walls and floors of black Sainte Anne marble.

Mulberry

**100 REGENT STREET,
SOHO**

British entrepreneur Roger Saul named his luxury leathergoods brand after the mulberry trees he used to walk past on his way to school in Somerset. The idea for the label came from a conversation at his kitchen table, and his sister designed the pretty mulberry tree logo. Mulberry is now the largest manufacturer of luxury leather goods in the UK, known for their iconic English satchel bags, especially after the immense success of their collaboration with the uber stylish Alexa Chung. The Mulberry store on Regent Street was designed by Faye Toogood as a tribute to the

British landscape – in moody blues, deep greens and pale pinks. Polished concrete contrasts with rich velvet furnishings, and the space is dotted with hand-tufted rugs and dramatic abstract paintings that reflect the brand's modern British identity.

MULBERRY

Victoria Beckham

36 DOVER STREET, MAYFAIR

Polish your wardrobe with a visit to the Victoria Beckham flagship store in Mayfair's fashion mecca. It's an expansive, gallery-like space with clean geometric lines, contemporary concrete and reflective stainless steel. Victoria Beckham began her line in 2008 with a collection of fitted dresses and now makes both high fashion and ready-to-wear, often reflecting her own distinctive personal style. Her romantic floral blouses, androgynous tailoring and body-shaping compact knits are made to fit women's daily lives of work, socialising and of course travel.

VICTORIA BECKHAM

Simone Rocha

93 MOUNT STREET, MAYFAIR

With pearls and lace alongside straps and plastic, Simone Rocha's style is part princess, part punk, and there's a fierce toughness stitched in with her flowing feminine silhouettes. Simone debuted at London Fashion Week in September 2010 and has been showing there ever since. She's been worn by style icons like Gillian Anderson and Rihanna, designed a

Simone Rocha

sell-out collection for H&M and shown at the Tate Modern. Her prestigious stockists include Bergdorf Goodman in New York and of course Harrods here in London, while her minimalist Mayfair boutique is decorated with her own sculptures and displays her designs on Perspex plinths.

Simone

Temperley London

163 DRAYCOTT AVENUE, CHELSEA

Temperley London's flagship is an intricately decorated black Georgian townhouse, with 'Temperley' curling in shining gold script over the display window. Inside, traditional details like bevel-edged mirrors and brass hanging rails create a fitting backdrop for Alice Temperley's feminine, playful and decadent style. Her love of sweet romantic florals and the English countryside can be seen in her designs, including Temperley Bridal (located on the first floor), as well as her collaboration with British stationery brand Papier.

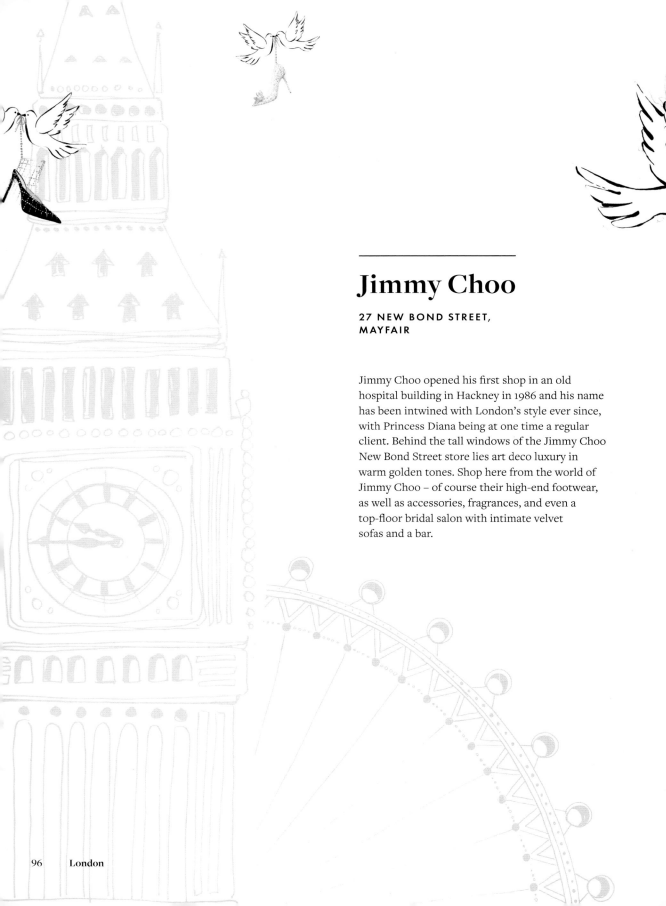

Jimmy Choo

27 NEW BOND STREET, MAYFAIR

Jimmy Choo opened his first shop in an old hospital building in Hackney in 1986 and his name has been intwined with London's style ever since, with Princess Diana being at one time a regular client. Behind the tall windows of the Jimmy Choo New Bond Street store lies art deco luxury in warm golden tones. Shop here from the world of Jimmy Choo – of course their high-end footwear, as well as accessories, fragrances, and even a top-floor bridal salon with intimate velvet sofas and a bar.

JIMMY CHOO

Paul Smith

40–44 FLORAL STREET, COVENT GARDEN

With his instantly recognisable colourful stripe logo, Paul Smith now operates a leading British independent design firm. Their flagship is on Floral Street, a lovely narrow cobbled avenue lined with several high-end shops. Number 40 was once a little old bakery before Paul Smith transformed it into his first London store, opening in 1979. The store is dotted with eclectic artworks and curios, and offers an in-house monogramming service as well as alterations in their suit room. Lovers of Paul Smith might also visit their Mayfair shop, which houses temporary art exhibitions, or even book a night in the bright suite at Brown's Hotel designed and curated by Paul Smith.

JW Anderson

**2 BREWER STREET,
SOHO**

JW Anderson's flagship store has an aesthetic that suits the playful, contemporary look of this luxury clothing brand. JW Anderson shot to attention in the UK with his Topshop collaboration in 2012, and has been winning British Fashion Awards ever since. Anderson is always experimenting with his gender-defying androgynous style, putting skirts on men and sports suits on women. You're sure to see something distinctive and exciting in his Soho store, which features industrial window dressings and neon signage, paying tribute to the borough's famous nightlife.

JWANDERSON

NDERSON

Chanel

**158–159 NEW
BOND STREET,
MAYFAIR**

Coco Chanel once said, 'Fashion is not something that exists in dresses only. Fashion is in the sky, in the street, fashion has to do with ideas, the way we live, what is happening.' While she likely had Paris in mind, I think this quote certainly applies to the streets of London. Chanel's London flagship store on New Bond Street holds commissioned artworks inspired by Coco's Paris apartment and features a larger-than-life sculpture of her emblematic strands of pearls. More pearls are hand-stitched into the changing room curtains, while the marble staircase and white crystal chandeliers are the epitome of luxury. Chanel's ready-to-wear, jewellery, beauty, leather goods, watch, shoe and accessories collections are immaculately displayed throughout.

Dior

**160–162
NEW BOND STREET,
MAYFAIR**

The Dior Maison on New Bond Street is their largest UK store and was designed by celebrated architect Peter Marino. Inside, it feels like a Parisian hôtel, with silk carpets and neo-Louis XVI furniture, all in a palette of Dior grey, pale turquoise and pink. The store is a temple to art and design, featuring lamps by Belgian designer Wouter Hoste, a sculpture from American artist Nick van Woert, and furniture by the likes of French sculptor Claude Lalanne. An animated mural by visual artist Oyoram lights up the marble staircase that connects the store's departments: men's, women's, baby and childrenswear, homewares, their wonderful shoe gallery and the luxurious VIP shopping salons.

Manolo Blahnik

**49–51 OLD CHURCH STREET,
CHELSEA**

Manolo Blahnik's designs are timeless. The story is
that when Blahnik was studying art and set design
in Paris, fashion legend Diana Vreeland was looking
over his sketches for *A Midsummer Night's Dream*.
She spotted his design for Hippolyta's high-heeled
sandal and directed him to focus on making shoes.
And aren't we glad he did? When I think of Manolo
Blahnik, I can't help seeing Carrie Bradshaw walking
the streets of New York in *Sex and the City*, but his
feminine designs are no less at home in this beautiful
city. Visit his first ever boutique in Chelsea, which was
established in 1970, to see his current collections and
appreciate his attention to detail and stylish flair.

bamford

Bamford

**104 DRAYCOTT AVENUE,
BROMPTON CROSS**

Bamford's spa and flagship store in Brompton Cross
is a haven designed to reflect its beginnings in the
beautiful landscape of the Cotswolds – all marbles,
clay and pale timber. Each of the three floors is
dedicated to one of Bamford's core philosophies:
move, breathe and heal. The store has a yoga and
movement studio, tranquil treatment rooms and
a retail space with clothing, homewares and the
skincare, bath and body products that first brought
them public attention. I covet their luxurious clothing
line, which is all about heritage craftsmanship,
organic fabrics and flowing shapes inspired by
the natural world.

bamford

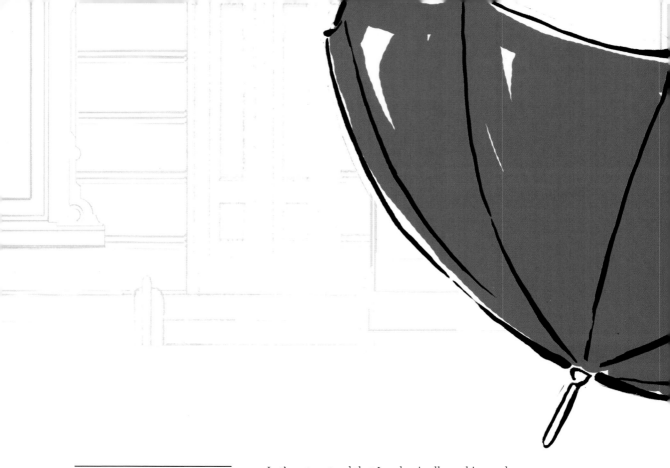

Hunter

SELFRIDGES
400 OXFORD STREET,
MARYLEBONE

HARRODS
87–135 BROMPTON ROAD,
KNIGHTSBRIDGE

Let's not pretend that London is all sunshine and clear days. Sometimes we all need a pair of puddle-proof boots with timeless style for exploring rain-washed streets – or possibly for dancing through the fields of Glastonbury Festival. Hunter have been making what Londoners call 'Wellington boots' since 1856. In more recent years they've been seen on style drivers like Alexa Chung, Kate Moss, and Cara Delevingne. Hunter even did a collaboration with the Langham Hotel to make cotton-candy pink boots in the luxury hotel's signature shade of Pantone 706C. For all your local outerwear needs – brollies, macs, and of course knee-high waterproof boots, you can browse the Hunter range at either Selfridges or Harrods.

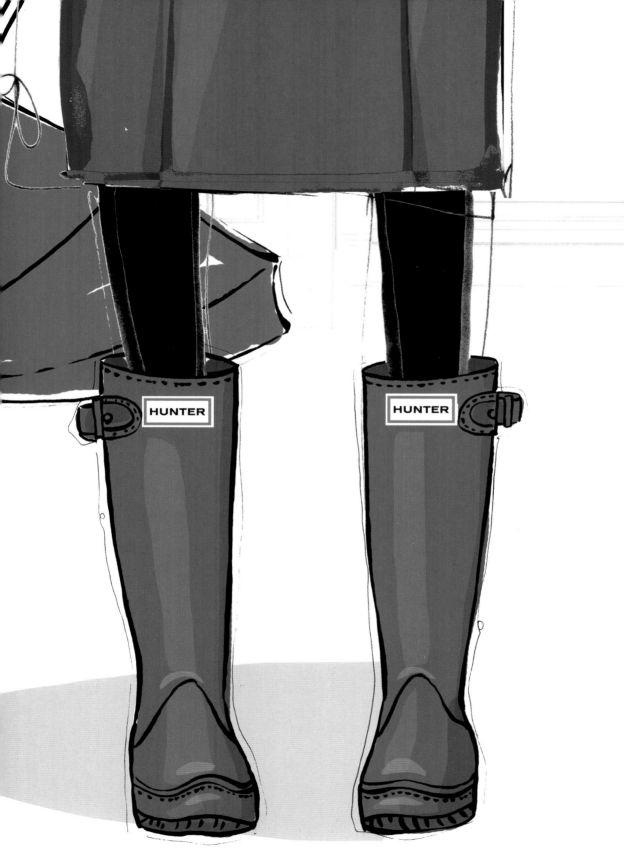

Needle
& Thread

**HARRODS 87–135
BROMPTON ROAD,
KNIGHTSBRIDGE**

**SELFRIDGES
400 OXFORD STREET,
MARYLEBONE**

Needle & Thread epitomise a kind of English rose
prettiness that makes my heart skip and I have now
lost count of just how many of their dresses I own!
Inspired by delicate florals and vintage fabrics, their
pieces feature feminine silhouettes, floating fabrics
and intricate embellishments of smocking, ruffles and
lace. The company, founded by Hannah Coffin in 2013,
also has a strong emphasis on sustainability. Look
for their dreamy dresses at Harrods or Selfridges to
embrace your own cottage-garden style or to feel
like a princess at your next special event.

Maison
Assouline

**196A PICCADILLY,
ST JAMES'S**

Maison Assouline sell their exclusive art books alongside everything you could need to fit out an elegant home library or studio. From gorgeous little notecards or scented candles to the perfect armchair, Maison Assouline offer all the accoutrements to help you bring a bit of London luxury back to your own home. Just off the hustle and bustle of Piccadilly, Assouline's stately showroom is a place to slow down, flip through some beautiful pages and allow inspiration to arrive. In need of refreshment? Step into Swans Bar for nibbles or cocktails and enjoy a selection of spirits as fine and rare as their books.

Lock & Co. Hatters

**6 ST JAMES'S STREET,
ST. JAMES'S**

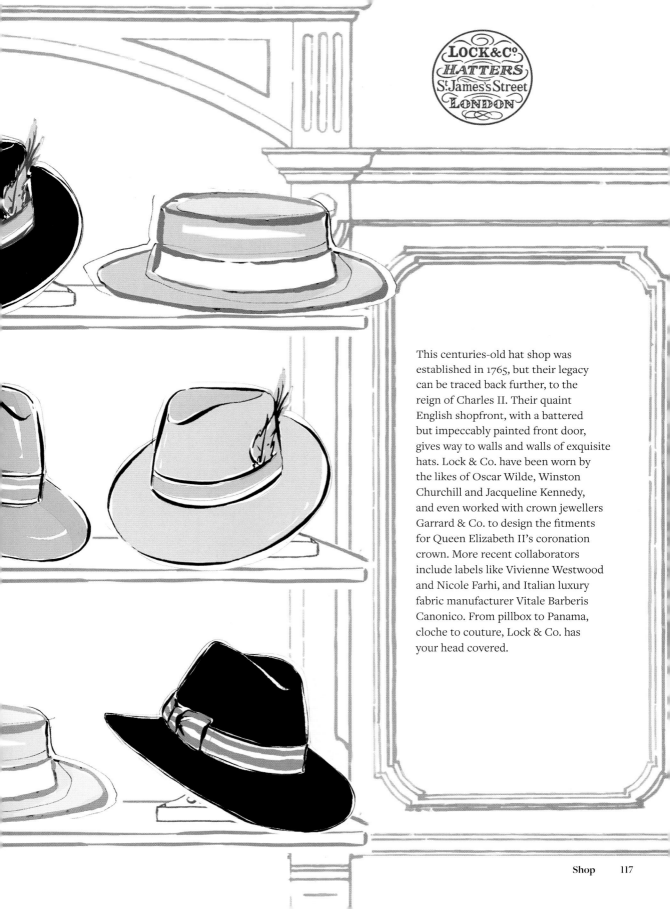

LOCK & Cº.
HATTERS
St James's Street
LONDON

This centuries-old hat shop was established in 1765, but their legacy can be traced back further, to the reign of Charles II. Their quaint English shopfront, with a battered but impeccably painted front door, gives way to walls and walls of exquisite hats. Lock & Co. have been worn by the likes of Oscar Wilde, Winston Churchill and Jacqueline Kennedy, and even worked with crown jewellers Garrard & Co. to design the fitments for Queen Elizabeth II's coronation crown. More recent collaborators include labels like Vivienne Westwood and Nicole Farhi, and Italian luxury fabric manufacturer Vitale Barberis Canonico. From pillbox to Panama, cloche to couture, Lock & Co. has your head covered.

Floris
London

**89 JERMYN STREET,
ST JAMES'S**

Floris of London perfumery was founded in 1730 by
Juan Famenias Floris and has been run by his family
ever since. The quintessentially English heritage
shopfront opens into a space that features Spanish
mahogany and glass display fittings taken from the
Crystal Palace of 1851's Great Exhibition. Floris has
sold their aromatic wares to customers ranging from
Marylin Munroe and the Royal Family, not to mention
Ian Fleming's James Bond, who is known for wearing
their No. 89 Eau de Toilette. If you love jewel-like
bottles filled with fragrances with notes of citrus
and musk, marine and mineral, or flora and herb,
this is a must-visit on your London calendar.

Wedgwood

HARRODS
87–135 BROMPTON ROAD,
KNIGHTSBRIDGE

SELFRIDGES
400 OXFORD STREET,
MARYLEBONE

Founded in 1759 by Josiah Wedgwood, this distinctive brand became known for its exquisite tea sets and fine bone china, which have been used to entertain guests in elegant homes across England for centuries. Wedgwood is synonymous with the tradition of afternoon tea – taken with delicate sandwiches, pretty cakes and fluffy scones. You can discover Wedgwood pieces both in Harrods and Selfridges, or, if you're headed to the West Midlands, stop in at the World of Wedgwood near Stoke-on-Trent to marvel at their timeless designs and unparalleled craftsmanship.

Smythson

131–132 NEW BOND STREET, MAYFAIR

Who doesn't love the smell of fresh paper, and the feel of embossed leather and soft ribbon page markers? Frank Smythson opened his first boutique on New Bond Street in 1887, selling stationery and carefully handcrafted 'fancy articles of a high-class character'. The store holds several Royal Warrants and previous customers include Vivien Leigh and Grace Kelly. There's even a tiny museum at the back of their flagship store where you can see Katharine Hepburn's engraved address book. I love their luxurious notebooks, but you can also embrace the modern world with their stylish phone covers. Smythson also has boutiques on Sloane Street and Westbourne Grove, as well as Heathrow Airport for that last-minute gift purchase.

Penhaligon's

**41 WELLINGTON STREET,
COVENT GARDEN**

William Penhaligon was appointed Royal Barber and Perfumer to the Royal Court in the Victorian era. There are now several Penhaligon's boutiques in London where you can find their decadent scents, but the 'most Penhaligon of all' is the oldest, in Covent Garden. Beyond the antique black-and-gold storefront, you'll find glass display cases glittering with precious bottles of fragrance, topped with the classic round glass stopper, or the galvanised gold creatures that signify their portrait range. For the full experience, book a fragrance profiling appointment and talk with an expert who will help you match with your perfect scent.

Twinings

216 STRAND,
TEMPLE

What could be more English than a fragrant, steaming cup of tea? And possibly the most English tea is Twinings. In 1837 Queen Victoria granted Twinings their first Royal Warrant, a distinction that every monarch since has upheld. Directly opposite the Royal Courts of Justice on the Strand, the Twinings flagship store proudly displays their golden logo and coat of arms above the door. Here you can try samples at their loose-leaf bar, or curate your own personal collection of individually wrapped tea bags from their pick-and-mix wall, to store in a deluxe Twinings wooden box. Tea devotees might even book themselves into a 'classic tea masterclass' or a 'bespoke blending session', to learn a little more about their passion.

The Apple Market

COVENT GARDEN

Covent Garden Apple Market was once a world-famous fruit and vegetable market. Now it's bustling with makers, buyers and sellers of one-off art, jewellery and other trinkets, below its glass roof and soaring wrought-iron arches. From the Apple Market, you can continue to explore the charm and vibrancy of London's historic market scene. Not far away, the East Colonnade Market sells goods, such as handmade soaps and hand-knitted children's clothes, and the Jubilee Market has a rotating schedule of wares, from antiques to crafts.

MARKET

ANTIQUES

TAGE FASHION

URNITURE DESIGN

OLD SPITALFIELDS MARKET

Old Spitalfields Market

16 HORNER SQUARE, SPITALFIELDS

Located in the heart of East London, Old Spitalfields Market dates back to 1638, when it was first licensed by King Charles I as a place to sell produce. This historic landmark is now a vibrant, sprawling covered market that houses a variety of independent stallholders, selling everything from antiques and flowers to vintage fashion and street food. As well as the daily market, there is a regular arts markets, and a style market with clothing and accessories from independent designers. Check their schedule and come in to trawl for one-of-a-kind fashion pieces and other unique treasures. Just don't get confused and end up at the New Spitalfields Market in Leyton, unless you're planning to buy wholesale fresh produce and flowers!

Portobello
Road Market

NOTTING HILL

Portobello Road Market meanders for a mile along Portobello Road from Notting Hill Gate and around the corner into Golborne Road. It's one of the world's most famous street markets and is always packed, especially during the Saturday antique market,

with crowds hunting for treasures beneath rows of marquees. Beside it, Portobello Green is home to a vintage clothing market, full of retro fashion, specialist stalls and handcrafted items. Wander around the surrounding Notting Hill area to gaze at the pretty pastel Victorian terraces, and perhaps pretend you are Julia Roberts looking for Hugh Grant. Designers Bella Freud and Stella McCartney have both lived nearby, so you never know who you might spot.

Oxford Street

···········

WESTMINSTER

In the 1800s Oxford Street was known as 'Ladies' Mile', because it was one of the few places considered acceptable for upper-class women to shop unaccompanied. Now, an average of half a million people visit Oxford Street every day. It's a thriving shopping district, lined with the flagship stores of high-street brands. You won't be able to miss the wonderful façade of Selfridges luxury department store or the very British Marks & Spencer. With Hyde Park and Marble Arch at one end, Mayfair just around the corner, and the embassy district of Grosvenor Square nearby, Oxford Street is right in the middle of such stunning London architecture. I never get tired of watching the endless stream of iconic red London busses trundle down the busy street.

New Bond Street

MAYFAIR

New Bond Street has been synonymous with luxury shopping since the 1700s, with stately Georgian buildings lining the footpath. It's a wonderful place just to wander and enjoy the sumptuous window displays. You'll find boutiques for Chanel, Dior, Jimmy Choo and Smythson, which all have their own entries in this book, as well as

other prestigious brands like Cartier, Dolce & Gabbana, Hermès, Louis Vuitton, Prada and the Ralph Lauren flagship with its blue-and-gold awnings. New Bond Street is also home to high-end jewellery boutiques and art galleries, as well as Sotheby's and Bonhams – two of the world's premier auctioneers of fine art and antiques. In July the street comes to life with Art in Mayfair, celebrating art, fashion and culture in collaboration with the Royal Academy of Arts.

Savile Row

MAYFAIR

When I first lived in London, my work brought
me to Savile Row, the epicentre of British tailoring
excellence. It was incredible to access some of the
private back rooms and gain an insight into this
historic world. The walnut wood, leather couches,
and giant stately bookshelves are the perfect setting
for the expert craftsmanship that has been practised
here for hundreds of years. The dinner jacket was
first created by Savile Row tailor Henry Poole, and
the term 'bespoke' was first used here to mean
custom-made, by hand. Illustrious clients of Savile
Row range from Lord Nelson and Winston Churchill
to Mick Jagger and Jude Law. It's an unmissable
stop for any stylish gentleman.

Regent Street

MAYFAIR

Regent Street is one of the most iconic shopping destinations in London. Its sweeping curve of stately white-grey Portland stone buildings feature impressive façades and eye-catching window displays, blending historic charm with contemporary style. It is home to a wide range of luxury fashion brands such as Tory Burch and Burberry, as well as London's famous Liberty department store. Regent Street has a program of events, including Summer Streets, where the road is closed to traffic, and the special evening when they switch on their dazzling Christmas lights.

BURBERRY
LONDON

REGENT ST

ALLIANC

SLOANE
STREET

Sloane Street

CHELSEA

Sloane Street is dotted with elegant townhouses and charming English gardens. The flagship stores of some of the world's most prominent luxury brands line this street – Tom Ford, Chloé, Alberta Ferretti, Gucci and many more. The area is synonymous with high-end shopping, with Harvey Nichols at the north end of Sloane Street and Harrods not far away. In the 1980s, Princess Diana epitomised the sleek Sloane Street look, a certain effortless style associated the distinguished residents of nearby Sloane Square. Wander the neighbouring streets to find stunning Victorian mansion blocks and the white stucco-fronted houses that are characteristic of the local architecture.

Princes Arcade and Piccadilly Arcade

ST JAMES'S

London is full of secret pathways and lovely cobbled lanes to discover, and one of the things I adore on a wet day is exploring London's beautiful arcades. Princes Arcade connects Piccadilly with Jermyn Street and contains a curated little collection of boutiques, including hatters, shoe stores and menswear, not to mention Prestat, purveyors of fine chocolate to the Royal Family. As I walk down the arcade, I like looking up at the little signs hanging from their matching delicate scrollwork above each store window. Parallel to Princes Arcade, and directly across from the Royal Academy of Arts, is the curving glass entryway to Piccadilly Arcade. The brass lanterns and domed ceiling features, with their multitude of little windowpanes, lend Edwardian splendour to this aisle of jewellers, perfumers, shoemakers and menswear.

Vintage shopping

If you love foraging for hidden gems, London has a whole world of vintage fashion to lose yourself in. Brick Lane is lined with wonderful vintage stores – try Rokit, which began as a stall in Camden Market. Just around the corner on Cheshire Street, House of Vintage carefully curates rare pieces of men's and women's wear. As well as its incredible market, Portobello Road is a vintage shopper's paradise. Take a peek into Found And Vision, the luxury vintage store that boasts clients like Kate Moss and Bella Hadid and has even launched its own magazine. Annie's Ibiza in London's West End is also worth a visit to find an incredible mix of eclectic and rare, high-end pieces, carefully sourced from around the world.

3

Sleep

The Lanesborough

2 LANESBOROUGH PLACE,
KNIGHTSBRIDGE

Illustrating for The Lanesborough as their artist-in-residence has been one the highlights of my career. This immaculately renovated townhouse is a visual delight with its grand neo-classical façade and opulent rooms. In 1719, James Lane, second and last Viscount Lanesborough, built a residence on this site, but the current structure was built in the 1870s as a hospital.

In 1991, it reopened its fabulous doors as a hotel and soon became beloved of the glamorous elite. Joan Collins, Mariah Carey and and Madonna have all made themselves at home here. If your budget doesn't quite stretch to staying in these luxurious rooms – each of which comes with its very own butler – you could visit for a heavenly spa or decadent afternoon tea.

Claridge's

BROOK STREET,
MAYFAIR

Claridge's is a London institution, founded in the 1850s and quickly becoming the favoured guesthouse of royalty. The current grand building, fitted out in a mix of gilt Art Deco glamour and traditional elegance, was designed by C. W. Stephens, architect of Harrods and Harvey Nichols. In the 1950s, Hollywood stars such as Cary Grant, Katharine Hepburn and Audrey Hepburn all stayed at Claridge's when they were in London. Actor Spencer Tracy apparently proclaimed that when he died, he'd rather go to Claridge's than to heaven. Since then, it hasn't lost its charm for the A-list crowd, and no wonder – its suites, restaurants and bars are the epitome of understated luxury.

The Connaught

16 CARLOS PLACE, MAYFAIR

This genteel Mayfair hotel is in an ideal location, less than a ten-minute walk to Hyde Park to the east and Bond Street's luxury shopping to the west. Inside, gleaming walnut and mahogany meet modern-day elegance with soft furnishings in muted greys and pale blues. The Connaught is like an art gallery, and a visitor could spend hours enjoying the wonderfully curated selection of original

artworks that adorn the walls. When Ralph Lauren visited, he loved the lobby staircase so much that he had it recreated for his Madison Avenue flagship store in New York. Interior designer extraordinaries David Collins and Guy Oliver were appointed for the room refurbishments, having also between them designed spaces for Harrods, Jimmy Choo and even 10 Downing Street.

The Ritz London

Famous hotelier César Ritz planned for his new hotel to be the most luxurious in the country. When The Ritz opened its doors in 1906, it was clear that he succeeded – so much so that the hotel was the origin of the word 'ritzy', to mean ostentatiously fashionable or stylish. Anna Pavlova, the Russian prima ballerina, danced at the Ritz in 1912, Charlie Chaplin escaped his unruly fans here in 1921, and Jackie Onassis herself said The Ritz was 'like paradise'. Scenes from the classic romantic comedy *Notting Hill* and very English period drama *Downton Abbey* were filmed in and around the hotel.

The Savoy

STRAND,
WESTMINSTER

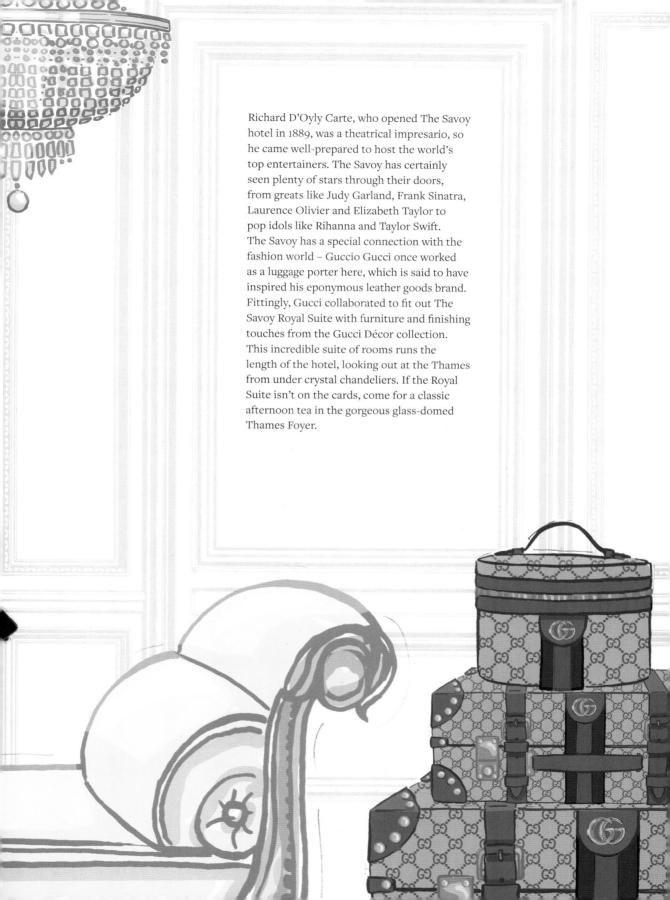

Richard D'Oyly Carte, who opened The Savoy hotel in 1889, was a theatrical impresario, so he came well-prepared to host the world's top entertainers. The Savoy has certainly seen plenty of stars through their doors, from greats like Judy Garland, Frank Sinatra, Laurence Olivier and Elizabeth Taylor to pop idols like Rihanna and Taylor Swift. The Savoy has a special connection with the fashion world – Guccio Gucci once worked as a luggage porter here, which is said to have inspired his eponymous leather goods brand. Fittingly, Gucci collaborated to fit out The Savoy Royal Suite with furniture and finishing touches from the Gucci Décor collection. This incredible suite of rooms runs the length of the hotel, looking out at the Thames from under crystal chandeliers. If the Royal Suite isn't on the cards, come for a classic afternoon tea in the gorgeous glass-domed Thames Foyer.

Brown's Hotel

33 ALBEMARLE STREET,
MAYFAIR

Queen Elizabeth II came to Brown's for afternoon tea, and they boast an extraordinary guestlist of literary greats – Rudyard Kipling famously wrote *The Jungle Book* here. This row of grand old Georgian townhouses was transformed into a sumptuous British hotel in 1837. Designer Olga Polizzi was part of the 2019 renovation, including incredible bespoke wallpapers which transform the rooms into fantasy gardens and jungles. One suite, in collaboration with Paul Smith, has a banana doorhandle, a wall hung with hand-picked artwork, and is dotted with his signature stripy cushions. Try their Donovan Bar for cocktails or Charlie's restaurant for a riff on traditional English fare.

The Dorchester

53 PARK LANE, MAYFAIR

The grand sweeping curve and wrought-iron balconies of The Dorchester look out over the wide green expanse of Hyde Park. Once the site of the American Embassy, this luxury hotel is home to a sumptuous spa and several bars and restaurants, including French chef Alain Ducasse's Michelin-starred restaurant. Afternoon tea is served every day in the Promenade – a long coral-pink room lined with gilt-topped columns, art and lush floristry. Some of the suites were designed in the 1950s by the artist and theatre designer Oliver Messel, featuring exquisite English floral fabrics and stately bookcases. From the 1930s, Foyles bookshop held their famous literary luncheons in The Ballroom, always attracting an illustrious crowd.

The Langham

**1C PORTLAND PLACE,
MARYLEBONE**

Staying at The Langham is like having your own castle in the middle of London, with plenty of georgous pink touches. It was built in 1865 as one of Europe's luxury Grand Hotels, and is located right next to the glittering delights of Regent Street. Sir Arthur Conan Doyle was a guest and set several *Sherlock Holmes* stories at the Langham. It was home to Mrs Wallis Simpson while she conducted her infamous affair with Edward VIII, which led to his abdication. During World War II the building hosted soldiers and a first aid post, then the BBC owned it for twenty years,

THE LANGHAM

storing their records in the vast ballroom. In 1991 Hilton returned the Langham to its original grandeur and hosted guests like Princess Diana and Cindy Crawford. The Langham's Artesian bar serves wonderful cocktails and Palm Court is perfect for an English afternoon tea.

Mandarin Oriental Hyde Park

....

66 KNIGHTSBRIDGE, KNIGHTSBRIDGE

The idea of sleeping like a princess in a turret suite overlooking Hyde Park is utterly charming to me. This Edwardian hotel even has a special grand entrance from the park, reserved only for royalty. (Don't worry, the rest of us are allowed to enter via the Knightsbridge side.) This was once the Hyde Park Hotel and was reopened in 2000 as the Mandarin Oriental. Glamorous entertainers have stayed here for more than a hundred years, from Rudolph Valentino and Shirley Bassey to Morgan Freeman. It's also home to the celebrated Dinner by Heston Blumenthal restaurant, with two Michelin stars, where you can try the famous chef's imaginative gastronomic creations.

Bulgari
Hotel
London

**171 KNIGHTSBRIDGE,
KNIGHTSBRIDGE**

I knew the Bulgari brand first as the magical
Roman jewellers whose tastefully elegant
pieces have been worn by stars like Ingrid
Bergman and Elizabeth Taylor. As you might
expect, Bulgari's London hotel, built in 2012,
is a gleaming contemporary masterpiece,
themed around precious silver. Bulgari's
expert craftsmanship is visible in all the
little finishing touches, both here and at
their expanding group of beautiful hotels
across the world. The London hotel is home
to a cigar shop, a cinema and the utterly
luxurious Bulgari Spa, with a curated range
of beauty and health treatments and a
shimmering swimming pool.

4

Eat/
Drink

Red Room

THE CONNAUGHT, 16 CARLOS PLACE, MAYFAIR

Pushing past a red velvet curtain in the Champagne Room at The Connaught hotel, you enter the almost secret Red Room. The space is like a rosy cave, with glittering glass panelling designed by Irish interior maestro Bryan O'Sullivan and artworks almost all by women, featuring Jenny Holzer, Ti-a Thuy Nguyen and Trina McKillen. There is something delicious about watching the marble drinks trolley arrive, delivering exquisite cocktails to your table, and British cheeses and oysters pair beautifully with the fine wine list.

The Painter's Room

CLARIDGE'S,
BROOK STREET,
MAYFAIR

The Painter's Room was designed as a tribute to Art Deco Europe by Bryan O'Sullivan, who was inspired by 1930s photographs of the space. Themed in pale blush, peach and cream, it features an astonishing pink onyx bar and an original stained-glass mural by British artist Annie Morris. Share plates pair with Mediterranean-inspired cocktails with original mixology and a curated selection of small-batch labels, perfect for enjoying beneath the domed skylight.

The Fumoir

**CLARIDGE'S,
BROOK STREET,
MAYFAIR**

Moody and intimate, The Fumoir was once thick with cigar smoke and has now been renovated in stunning Art Deco noir. This is a darkly glamorous bar, where impeccable glassware shines against leather stools, aubergine walls and gilt highlights. Some will come simply to appreciate the stunning Lalique crystal panels. Others will drop in for a coffee between shopping, or pre-theatre cocktails, or perhaps arrive after midnight to sip a final whiskey before bed.

The Library Bar

**THE LANESBOROUGH,
2 LANESBOROUGH PLACE,
KNIGHTSBRIDGE**

Sitting curled in a leather wing chair and sipping cocktails while a pianist plays in the background has got to be high on my list of quiet luxuries – and the pianist is a regular occurrence at The Lanseborough's Library Bar. I love the old-school elegance of this room lined with shelves of gold inlayed books, which give the space a sense of calm sophistication. The bar's menu leans towards lobster, foie gras and caviar, and its true specialty is its 'liquid museum' – there are cognacs here that date back to Napoleon! They also host a program of live music and other arts and literary experiences.

THE LANESBOROUGH
LONDON

LIBRARY BAR

The Lanesborough Grill

**THE LANESBOROUGH HOTEL,
2 LANESBOROUGH PLACE,
KNIGHTSBRIDGE**

Afternoon tea at the Lanesborough is served at their Grill, which is lit by a wonderful domed glass ceiling where the sun bounces off the dangling chandeliers. With tiered plates gracefully bearing soft sandwiches and sweet delicacies, fragrant tea in fine china teacups, or perhaps even an elderflower and jasmine daisy cocktail, this is afternoon tea at its exquisite British best. Book a table later in the evening for signature dishes such as beef wellington or coronation crab salad.

sketch

9 CONDUIT STREET, MAYFAIR

Is it a forest glade, or a three-starred Michelin restaurant? Standing on the mossy carpet, surrounded by magical greenery, I find it difficult to tell. This astonishing restaurant houses five different eateries, including the forest-like Glade, and the Gallery – a pink diner with walls lined with modern art. If you're dining in Mayfair and looking for an explosively contemporary aesthetic, this is the spot for you. Do not miss their bathrooms, with their enormous gleaming space-egg pods under a multicoloured glass ceiling.

CHANEL

Sexy Fish

BERKELEY SQUARE HOUSE, MAYFAIR

Vivid and outrageous, Sexy Fish deliver seafood dishes inspired by Japanese cuisine in an incredibly designed space. Water flows down the windows, mermaids and mirrored crocodiles emerge from the wall, and a DJ spins tunes for late-night visitors. Sexy Fish also offer private dining in their Coral Reef Room, where a gleaming aquarium lines one entire wall. Check for their dress code to make sure you look the part for this underwater fever dream.

The Tiffany Blue Box Cafe

HARRODS, ENTRANCE
OPPOSITE 22 HANS ROAD,
KNIGHTSBRIDGE

Co.

Who can forget Audrey Hepburn at dawn, wearing opulent pearls and that Givenchy black satin sheath as she gazes in at Tiffany's windows, nibbling a pastry? Now you can book your own breakfast at Tiffany's at the Blue Box Cafe at Harrods. Decorated in the iconic blue of that coveted Tiffany's box, with Tiffany-ware gracing the tables, the Blue Box Cafe is as elegant and well-appointed as you might expect. As well as breakfast, they also serve afternoon tea and cocktails. Bookings are only released on the second of each month, so this is one visit to plan early for a stylish meal to remember.

Baccarat Bar

HARRODS, ENTRANCE ON HANS CRESCENT, KNIGHTSBRIDGE

Even when Harrods department store is closed, there's a separate private entrance that opens for guests of the Baccarat Bar. This chandeliered subterranean cocoon of red leather and velvet has room for a very exclusive twenty-three guests. Baccarat's glittering crystal glassware takes centre stage, serving a cocktail list themed by colour. Food ranges from Oscietra caviar to burgers and truffle fries. Somehow, despite the chandeliers and marble floors, this bar manages to feel like a laid-back little hideaway to relax with friends.

Harry's
Dolce Vita

**27–31 BASIL STREET,
KNIGHTSBRIDGE**

Harry's Dolce Vita is a spin-off from Harry's Bar, a private members club in Mayfair. The restaurant is decked out in autumnal colours and inspired by the glamour of 1950s Italy. Federico Fellini's classic film *La Dolce Vita*, released in 1960, is set in a Rome of nightclubs, paparazzi and the luxury set, and is a milestone of sartorial style. Here, in Harry's version of Dolce Vita, I could almost be in one of the glamorous bars in that Fellini movie, and I certainly feel like I'm living 'the sweet life'. There is an entire Negroni menu here and the truffle pasta is an absolute must.

Le Pont de la Tour

36D SHAD THAMES, SOUTHWARK

Le Pont de la Tour is a sleek restaurant and bistro, with French cuisine and an extensive wine list. The nineteenth-century building is a former tea warehouse, now elegantly transformed for drinking and dining. A highlight of Le Pont de la Tour is its terrace along the Thames, with incredible views of the distinctive gothic turrets and high lattice walkway of London's Tower Bridge. Enjoy a wine while you watch the lights on the water on a balmy summer evening here, or if it's brisk, pull one of their fluffy blankets over your knees while you warm your hands around a coffee.

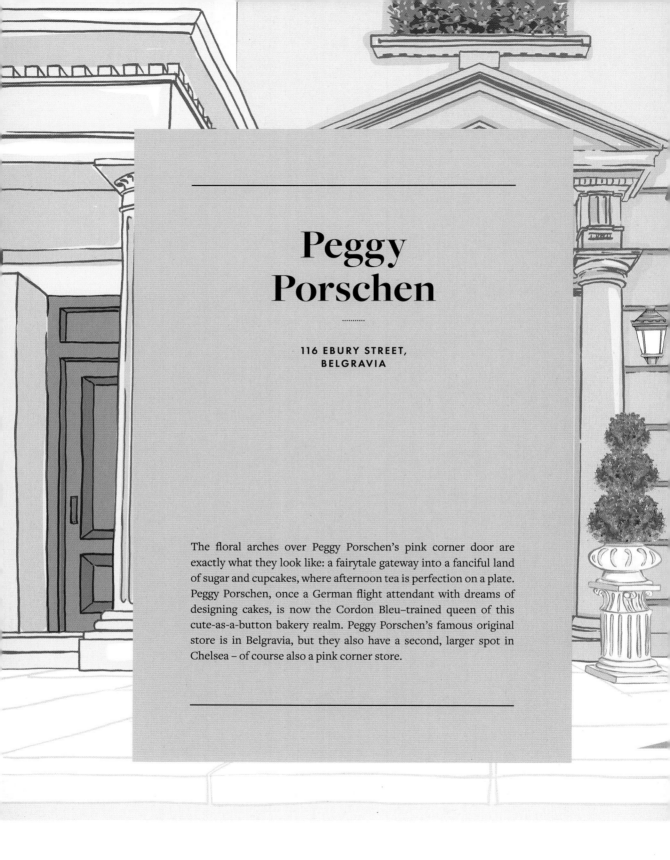

Peggy Porschen

···········

**116 EBURY STREET,
BELGRAVIA**

The floral arches over Peggy Porschen's pink corner door are exactly what they look like: a fairytale gateway into a fanciful land of sugar and cupcakes, where afternoon tea is perfection on a plate. Peggy Porschen, once a German flight attendant with dreams of designing cakes, is now the Cordon Bleu–trained queen of this cute-as-a-button bakery realm. Peggy Porschen's famous original store is in Belgravia, but they also have a second, larger spot in Chelsea – of course also a pink corner store.

Scott's

**20 MOUNT STREET,
MAYFAIR**

Scott's of Mayfair holds a special place in the heritage of fine dining in London. It began as an oyster warehouse in the 1800s and is renowned for its urbane ambiance and sophisticated market-fresh seafood menu. Scott's al fresco dining, with their signature black awning over the verdant terrace, is often frequented by paparazzi seeking snaps of the stars. Kate Moss and Victoria Beckham are known to dine here, and Scott's claim to have inspired James Bond's martini, 'shaken, not stirred'. For special events, their Renoir Room is available for private dining, with its luminous semi-precious green agate stone floor, which almost (not quite) outshines the collection of original art masterpieces hanging from the walls.

Isabel
Mayfair

....

**26
ALBEMARLE STREET,
MAYFAIR**

With silk panelled walls, hand-painted wallpaper, a mirrored ebony bar, and a sea of brightly polished brass lamps across the ceiling, Isabel combines the historic grandeur of Mayfair with the sophisticated joy of Latin America and the Mediterranean. The wait staff wear formal white coats, and the star-studded clientele make Isabel a wonderful place to drink champagne and people-watch. Come for brunch, or dinner, or even for late-night adventures, with the possibility that you might be admitted downstairs to their Dragon Room, an invite-only venue with a DJ skilfully mixing tunes under the mirrored ceiling.

The Ivy Chelsea Garden

195–197 KING'S ROAD, CHELSEA

THE IVY
CHELSEA GARDEN

The original Ivy sprang from an early 1900s Covent Garden cafe, which was popular with the flamboyant local theatre community. There are now several sumptuous Ivy restaurants across London. The Ivy Chelsea Garden serves their all-day menu in a gorgeous terrace garden and orangery, as well as a rich indoor space decorated with lush foliage. I particularly love sitting outside, amongst water features and overflowing pots of greenery, shaded by pergolas and wide umbrellas. The Ivy is known for their signature shepherd's pie, and there are plenty of vegetarian and vegan options too. Tables at the Ivy are highly sought after, so make your booking early.

Listings

Acknowledgements

To Emily Hart, for being my wonderful publisher on this book. Just one of many that we've created together. Thank you for making every single book such a joy to work on.

To Antonietta Anello, for editing and overseeing this book to perfection.

To Martina Granolic, thank you for deep diving into the best of London and pouring over every single entry in this book. Many of these wonderful places we've found together on our work adventures in London!

To Staci Barr, thank you for your incredible work and endless hours helping me bring the illustrated pages to life. You brought such skill and beauty to this book.

To Ailsa Wild, thank you for jumping into this book head first (although, you did once join the circus!) and find every single wonderful and inspiring detail about London.

To Missy Lewis, thank you for all your invaluable research into every beautiful London location in this book – it was the starting point for all that we discovered.

To Murray Batten, another book together and once again you've brought it to life with your incredible design and eye for detail.

To Todd Rechner, for your incredible care and attention in seeing my books to their finished form. You've made each book something precious to hold, to read, to keep forever. Thank you.

To my husband Craig and my children Gwyn and Will, thank you for always being ready for our next adventure!

About the author

Megan Hess was destined to draw. An initial career in graphic design evolved into art direction for some of the world's leading advertising agencies and for Liberty London. In 2008, Megan illustrated Candace Bushnell's number-one-bestselling book *Sex and the City*. This catapulted Megan onto the world stage, and she began illustrating portraits for *The New York Times*, *Vogue Italia*, *Vanity Fair* and *TIME*, who described Megan's work as 'love at first sight'.

Today, Megan is one of the world's most sought-after fashion illustrators, with a client list that includes Givenchy, Tiffany & Co., Valentino, Louis Vuitton and *Harper's Bazaar*. Megan's iconic style has been used in global campaigns for Fendi, Prada, Cartier, Dior and Salvatore Ferragamo. She has illustrated live for fashion shows such as Fendi at Milan Fashion Week, Chopard at the 2019 Cannes Film Festival, Viktor&Rolf and Christian Dior Couture.

Megan has created a signature look for Bergdorf Goodman, New York, and a bespoke bag collection for Harrods of London. She has illustrated a series of portraits for Michelle Obama, as well as portraits for Gwyneth Paltrow, Cate Blanchett and Nicole Kidman. She is also the Global Artist in Residence for the prestigious Oetker Hotel Collection.

Megan illustrates all her work with a custom Montblanc pen that she affectionately calls 'Monty'.

Megan has written and illustrated ten bestselling fashion books, as well as her much-loved series for children, *Claris: the Chicest Mouse in Paris*.

When she's not in her studio working, you'll find Megan perched in a cosy London cafe secretly drawing all the fabulous Londoners around her.

Visit Megan at meganhess.com

First published in 2024 by Hardie Grant Books, an imprint of Hardie Grant Publishing

Hardie Grant Books (Melbourne)
Building 1, 658 Church Street
Richmond, Victoria 3121

Hardie Grant Books (London)
5th & 6th Floors
52–54 Southwark Street
London SE1 1UN

hardiegrant.com/books

Hardie Grant acknowledges the Traditional Owners of the Country on which we work, the Wurundjeri People
of the Kulin Nation and the Gadigal People of the Eora Nation, and recognises their continuing connection
to the land, waters and culture. We pay our respects to their Elders past and present.

A catalogue record for this
book is available from the
National Library of Australia

London: Through a Fashion Eye
ISBN 978 1 74379 964 2
10 9 8 7 6 5 4 3 2 1

Publishing Director: Emily Hart, Roxy Ryan
Editor: Antonietta Anello
Researcher: Ailsa Wild
Designer: Murray Batten
Production Manager: Todd Rechner
Production Controller: Jessica Harvie

Colour reproduction by Splitting Image Colour Studio
Printed in China by Leo Paper Products LTD.

The paper this book is printed on is from FSC®-certified forests and
other sources. FSC® promotes environmentally responsible, socially
beneficial and economically viable management of the world's forests.